Not Just Your Mommy & Daddy's RELIGION
Why I'm A Baptist
for teens!

Kurt COPELAND

Copyright © 2017 Kurt Copeland
All rights reserved.
All Scripture quotations are taken from the King James Bible

All rights reserved. No part of this book may be reproduced, stored in a retrieval system, or transmitted in any form or by any means—electronic, mechanical, photocopy, recording, or otherwise—without written permission of the publisher, except for brief quotations in printed reviews.

Printed in the United States of America
Cover design and Layout: Amanda Stephan

ISBN-13: 978-1546496373

ACKNOWLEDGMENTS

For those who know me understand that a work like this certainly could not have happened without the advice, encouragement and help of so many. I am today what I am due to the influence and investment of so many in my past. It is the influence of those who have poured their life into me that has motivated me to put into print a book that can be a tool to help build the foundation of generations to follow.

To the teenagers of Franklin Road Baptist Church, I am so very grateful for your encouragement along the way. For allowing me to use you as the test subjects along the way listening me preach messages on these subjects. And lastly for your input on the title of the book—although some of the titles were a little odd . . . <u>Requirements for Marrying My Daughter</u>. I'm still trying to figure that one out!

To Michelle Cox and Janay Herting, thank you for the multiple editing sessions you had to fix all of my grammatical errors. I am sure editing is tough to begin with, but then add my writing and it becomes nearly impossible. Thank you for your labor of love and for your help with the FRBC youth ministry.

To Amanda Stephan, your work of publishing

this book has been a Godsend to me. Thank you for your advice and patience in working with me through the multiple changes and revamps of the book. You have been such an encouragement along the way to me.

To my friends Dr. Norris and Dr. Pope, I am humbled that you would put your name on this book in support of its contents and its author. I am thrilled to call Dr. Norris my pastor and my friend. I have had the honor of serving the Lord with you here at Franklin Road since 1999 and I wouldn't trade it for the world. Thank you for your genuine example and your love for our Saviour. Dr. Pope, your wisdom and influence across the nation for Christ is amazing. I am thankful for your foreword in this work. I consider both of you to be hero's in my life.

To my family, I am so blessed to call Angel Dawn and Gabby Daye my little ladies. I couldn't have handpicked two girls I would rather have as my daughters. You have put up with my corny youth pastor humor. Also, you have been wonderful to allow me to use you as examples in preaching as well as in this book. Christy, January 1, 1994, was the greatest day of my life outside of salvation— the day you said "I do" to me and became my wife and my biggest fan. I am the man I am because of you! I love all three of you ladies and am the most blessed man on earth because of you. You all have played a vital role in encouraging me in writing this book.

CONTENTS

	Introduction	
1	The Bible–God's Love Letter to Us	15
	A. A Matter of Faith	
	B. A Matter of Preservation	
	C. A Matter of Love	
2	The Autonomy of the Church–It Is Alive	27
	A. Importance of the Church	
	B. Formation of the Church	
	C. Leadership of the Church	
	D. Charge to the Church	
3	The Priesthood of Believers–I'm Somebody to God	43.
4	The Two Ordinances–My Obedience is So Important	53
	A. Baptism	
	B. Lord's Supper	
5	Individual Soul Liberty–We All Will Answer for Ourselves	67
	A. The Great White Throne Judgment	
	B. The Judgment Seat of Christ	
	C. The Choice	
6	Separation–Let People Know Who You Are	81
	A. Personal	
	B. Ecclesiastical	
7	The Two Offices–Follow the Leader	97
	A. Pastor	
	B. Deacons	
8	Salvation–God's Gift of Grace Through Faith Alone	109
9	Conclusion	117

FOREWORD

I have just read Kurt Copeland's *Not Just Your Mommy and Daddy's Religion: Why I Am a Baptist for Teenagers.* I am thankful for Kurt's willingness to write such a needful book, custom made for teens. According to Rainer Research, approximately 70 percent of American youth between the ages of 18 and 22 drop out of church. A few years ago Drew Dyck wrote an alarming article entitled, <u>The Leavers</u>, stating that more than in previous generations, 20- and 30-somethings are abandoning the faith. The studies point out that late teens and young adults who have "deconverted" (a chilling term that only recently is being used). When those interviewed repeatedly said that when they took their doubts to others in the church, they either received trite answers or were insulted for daring to ask.

I Peter 3:15 commands us to *"...be ready always to give an answer to every man that asketh you a reason of the hope that is in you with meekness and fear."* You hold in your hands a manual that tackles the essentials of our belief system as devout Bible believing Baptists. Our brother does so in concise, doctrinally spot on and yet down to earth teenage language that would be understandable by any teen in any Independent Baptist youth ministry.

I like to think of Kurt Copeland as a teen coach. A coach for a high school basketball team will train his players and teach them the plays and then go over them again and again. I recall our coach in my youth would call out "Four!" or "Two" or "One." Sometimes from the bench he would simply hold up the number of fingers designating the play. Immediately we would align ourselves on the court and set up the play in split second timing. Our victory was often determined by how well we knew and responded to the plays that were called.

The youth of today are being assaulted in spiritual warfare in such a way that, unless they know what they believe and why they believe, they will be numbered among the "leavers." I would encourage all of our youth ministries to study this book and these great doctrines of the Bible. I appreciate everything Brother Kurt addresses, especially his explanations of the two Baptist distinctives: "The Priesthood of Believers" and "Soul Liberty." I have never seen any writings dedicated to youth that deal with these very important doctrines. These distinctives have holding power and will do much to keep our tempted youth from going prodigal. It is easier to build up youth than to re-build broken adults.

There is a personal reason I recommend the writing of Kurt Copeland. Our youth pastor, Caleb Sargent is a product of Kurt's youth ministry at Franklin Road Baptist Church. Our youth pastor is a holy young man of God and for over half a decade has been a significant role model to our teens. From fourteen years of age until he left for Bible College, Brother Kurt Copeland was his mentor. At our church we have enjoyed, by proxy, the great wisdom, holiness and dedication reflected in the life and now the writing of Kurt Copeland. And this is not because our youth pastor borrowed this dedication from Kurt; it is because he owns these truths himself. And this is the true test of a man's ministry, when those who follow him are taught to follow Christ on their own. And now as our youth pastor coaches and calls out the plays, I hear the echo of his mentor, Brother Kurt Copeland. May God bless you as you read *Not Just Your Mommy and Daddy's Religion: Why I Am a Baptist for Teenagers*. I heartily recommend this book!

—Johnny Pope, Pastor of Christchurch Baptist Fellowship, Houston, Texas

INTRODUCTION

I am the product of Christian education. My parents enrolled my three older brothers and me in a small ACE Christian School when I was just in the third grade. I ultimately graduated from Franklin Road Christian School with a solid Bible-based Christian education. Our youth ministry spent nearly every Saturday morning out knocking on doors on teen soul-winning. Even with being raised in a great church and Christian education, there was always a fear in my heart of "what if the person behind the door asks me a tough question?" I felt so unprepared to answer even some basic Bible questions. So often we are content to just roll through life with "not knowing" instead of learning the basics.

It is so unfortunate that many times our teens will grow up in a Christian home, attend a solid, Bible-believing Baptist church, go through many years of Christian education, and STILL not know what they believe. It is my desire to help teens of our good churches to know why we call ourselves Baptists. There are so many different denominations in our nation today to the point that it can confuse and cause disillusionment to our teenagers. Many times, these same teens are the leaders of our churches. They are the ones teaching children's Sunday school classes, working on the bus routes, and serve as an army of door-knockers inviting others to Jesus.

Through the pages of this book, I want to help clear up some confusion and answer some questions on why we call ourselves Baptists. Some may say that it is not important to call yourself by one denomination or another; however, I believe strongly that the name *Baptist* actually points to what we believe. It also helps give clarity to those looking for a church, showing the beliefs of a particular church. A person ought to know what doctrine they will hear preached in a church service based on the name of the church. When I was a teenager while out on soul-winning, I had one man tell me that he would never go to my church simply because my pastor spent all his time preaching on "doctrine." I wish I knew then what I know now. The term *doctrine,* according to the Webster's Dictionary, literally means

1. teaching instruction
2. something that is taught
3. a principle or position or the body of principles in a branch of knowledge or system of belief: dogma

What is the Bible? It is the doctrine–or the teachings–of God. A church should be designed to teach us the Word of God.

In this introduction, I believe it is important to stress that our Baptist Distinctives are not to be confused with the six fundamentals of our faith. There are basic fundamental beliefs that are clearly presented in the Word of God which are called the Fundamentals of the Christian faith. These six doctrines are the basics of what makes us Baptists. These six teachings from the Word of God are vital for every teenager to not only know, but to also know why we believe them. In simple list format, the six fundamentals of the Baptist doctrine are as follows:

1. The Verbal Inspiration of the Word of God–2 Timothy 3:16-17; Psalm 119:89
2. The Vital Deity of Christ–Jesus is God–Philippians 2:5-11; Isaiah 53:1-6
3. The Virgin Birth of Christ–No sin nature–Matthew 1:23; Galatians 4:4
4. The Vicarious Suffering of Christ on the Cross–He paid my sin debt–I Peter 2:24; Hebrews 2:9
5. The Victorious Resurrection of Christ–Because He rose, so will we–John 11:25-26; I Corinthians 15:1-4, 20-22; John 14:19
6. The Visible Return of Jesus–He will return someday SOON–Acts 1:11; Revelation 1:7

These are the basic Bible fundamentals and are the basis for what we believe as Baptists. Within the six fundamentals of the faith listed above, you will find out the teachings that separate us from all the other denominations in our world today. Each of the fundamentals are vitally important in our faith; however, the Baptist Distinctives go deeper into what makes us not just a Baptist, but in particular, a Bible-believing, Independent Baptist.

For too long we have helped children know Christ as their Saviour, but we have not equipped and trained our next generation on what we believe and, just as important, why we believe what we believe. Use this text as a tool for reinforcing what you believe. Please take the time to carefully look up, study, and even memorize all the passages of Scripture referenced throughout these pages. Reinforce not only what you believe as a Baptist believer, but also learn why we believe it. We must not lose the next generation of teenagers. Our families, churches, nation and world need believers that know what they believe and why!

CHAPTER 1
THE BIBLE
God's Love Letter To Us

Why do we have a Bible? Who wrote the Bible? How do we know the Bible is true? Over the years, these are just a few questions that well-meaning teenagers have asked. These teenagers were not being critical, but were just inquisitive and hungry for answers. I believe this shows that there are more questions that are being asked internally. Many teens do not know who to turn to in order to get the answers to the questions they have. It is imperative that every teen understands that the Bible is the Word of God because it truly is the foundation to all the doctrines we teach. If someone does not believe the Word of God, he cannot go to Heaven, for it truly is the source of understanding salvation. The Bible teaches clearly that *"faith cometh by hearing, and hearing by the Word of God"*— Romans 10:17. I cannot stress enough the importance of placing our confidence in the Word of God.

The Bible contains sixty-six books divided into two sections: The Old Testament and the New Testament. The Old Testament contains thirty-nine books, while the New Testament has the remaining twenty-seven books. The Holy Spirit used forty different men with varied abilities and occupations to write the Word of God. From start to finish, it took 1,500 years to write the entire Word of God. There are many subjects covered in the Word of God, yet they flow in perfect harmony–this is a direct result of the fact that God truly is the Author of the Word of God. I understand that this is humanly impossible, but that is exactly what makes it the Word of God.

Not Just Your Mommy and Daddy's Religion

A MATTER OF FAITH

Let me say first of all, believing the Bible is God's Holy Word is a matter of faith. The Bible itself says in Hebrews 11:6 *"that without faith it is impossible to please God."* As a Baptist, we believe the Bible to be the inspired, inerrant Word of God. We hear the word *inspired* a lot in today's society. The song writer may say he was *inspired* to write a particular song. I do not doubt that song writer at all; however, the use of the word *inspired* for the song writer is vastly different than *inspired* dealing with the Word of God. The Song writer's *inspiration* refers to *idea* or *motivation*. II Timothy 3:16 states,

> *"All scripture is given by inspiration of God, and is profitable for doctrine, for reproof, for correction, for instruction in righteousness."*

This use of the word *inspiration* literally means "God-breathed." That means that God literally shared His Word with the writers of the Bible and allowed them the honor of writing God's Word. The book of Matthew is God's inspired Word, penned by the man named Matthew and influenced by his life. By faith we believe God used forty holy men of God to write God's words as He inspired them. II Peter 1:21 states,

"For the prophecy came not in old time by the will of man: but holy men of God spake as they were moved by the Holy Ghost."

The word *inerrant* means without error. This is God's perfect Word for us. Some would say that the Bible is full of errors and contradictions. That is a lie of Satan. After all, it was Satan that asked Eve in the Garden of Eden in Genesis 3:1, *"Hath God said?"* Satan's ultimate goal is to destroy God's Word and to convince mankind that it is not God's Word, but merely a historical book. Satan will attack in any way he can to discredit and destroy the Bible.

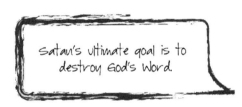

However, God's Word has stood the test of time and has had the power to change the lives of so many. God's Word has the power to save a soul, and to help a Christian lead a godly life for Him. Hebrews 4:12 confirms the power of the Word of God in our lives;

"For the word of God is quick, and powerful, and sharper than any twoedged sword, piercing even to the dividing asunder of soul

Not Just Your Mommy and Daddy's Religion

and spirit, and of the joints and marrow, and is a discerner of the thoughts and intents of the heart."

We must believe by faith that the Bible is God's Word.

A MATTER OF PRESERVATION

In our society today, there is so much confusion concerning the Word of God. There are so many types of "Bibles" to choose between. How do we know what Bible to use? I believe the answer is clear and simple. The debate really is between a simple choice–which original text is best? Without giving you an excuse to put this book down because it is too deep, here are some basic facts: Our modern day Bibles are translated from two basic sources. First, the King James Version is translated from the *Textus Receptus*, or *Received Text*, for the New Testament and from the Masoretic Text for the Old Testament. Most other versions of the Bible are translated from the *Westcott/Hort Text*. Here is the difference: the source of the Bible must be correct. We believe that the *Westcott/Hort* text would be an inferior text because of the many omissions of words and verses throughout the Bible as well as a host of changes to the Scriptures. Please do not fall into the lie of the Devil that says, "They are so similar, does it really matter?" God says not to change even *"one jot or one tittle"* of His Word according to Matthew 5:18. These other translations change what the Bible says. I challenge you to do a simple computer search that shows the changes and differences there are from one version of the Bible to another. As Independent Baptists, we believe the King James Bible is the inspired, preserved, perfect Word of God.

We believe that God has preserved His Word for us today. That simply means that God has used mankind throughout the ages to keep the Word of God pure and pass it down through the ages. We believe in the doctrine of preservation, just like we believe in the doctrine of inspiration. I Peter 1:25 says,

> *"But the word of the Lord endureth for ever. And this is the word which by the gospel is preached unto you."*

Matthew 24:35 says,

> *"Heaven and earth shall pass away, but my words shall not pass away."*

God definitely puts a high priority on His Word and is in the business of protecting it for us. I challenge you to memorize these other

Not Just Your Mommy and Daddy's Religion

passages of Scripture as well to increase your faith in the Word of God:

Deuteronomy 6:7-9–*"And these words, which I command thee this day, shall be in thine heart: And thou shalt teach them diligently unto thy children, and shalt talk of them when thou sittest in thine house, and when thou walkest by the way, and when thou liest down, and when thou risest up. And thou shalt bind them for a sign upon thine hand, and they shall be as frontlets between thine eyes. And thou shalt write them upon the posts of thy house, and on thy gates."*

Psalm 12:6-7–*"The words of the LORD are pure words: as silver tried in a furnace of earth, purified seven times. Thou shalt keep them, O LORD, thou shalt preserve them from this generation for ever."*

Psalm 119:89–*"For ever, O LORD, thy word is settled in heaven."*

Psalm 119:152–*"Concerning thy testimonies, I have known of old that thou hast founded them for ever."*

Psalm 119:160–*"Thy word is true from the beginning: and every one of thy righteous judgments endureth for ever."*

Isaiah 30:8–*"Now go, write it before them in a table, and note it in a book, that it may be for the time to come for ever and ever:"*

Isaiah 40:8–*"The grass withereth, the flower fadeth: but the word of our God shall stand for ever."*

A MATTER OF LOVE

Teenager, you can know and understand the Word of God. God's desire is that all of us get into His Word–learn it, memorize it, and practice it. It is God's love letter to you! God desires you to have a relationship with Him, and the only way to get to know God is through His Word. Read it daily, study it, learn it, and practice it.

I am reminded of the love letters I received from my wife before we were married. Wow! Did I ever treasure them! I would read them over and over again. I not only loved what she said in those love letters and notes, but I also loved how they smelled. Christy would put just a dab of her perfume on those notes, and I really loved to hold those notes and letters up to my nose and breathe in the "love" as well. I remember at college getting notes and letters

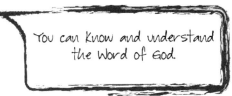
You can know and understand the Word of God.

Not Just Your Mommy and Daddy's Religion

from her. We were engaged to be married, and I loved to hear anything from her. After I read, re-read, and re-read again those letters, I would put them under my pillow of my dormitory bed–I never could get enough of Christy! I looked forward to spending that time with her through those love letters. I still get many love letters from my wife, and I save every one of them. They are so special to me. Unfortunately, I was guilty of desiring to read those love letters more than the one God had written to me. God's desire is to grow and develop a personal relationship with you, and His main avenue of developing that relationship with you is through His Holy Word.

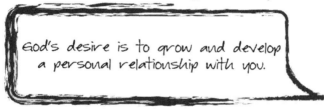

God's desire is to grow and develop a personal relationship with you.

God's Word is His love letter to you–do you treasure it? Let me ask you today, teenager, is your relationship with God growing or stagnant? Let me ask it a little more pointed: are you spending time with God daily in the Word of God? We say we believe the Bible is God's Holy Word, but I am confident that we really do not believe that to be true, simply because we do not practice what we say we believe. Think about it (don't hurt yourself though), you have the only letter that God has ever sent to man, and it is from the Creator of the world, yet we hardly spend much time, if any, reading that special letter! One of my favorite songs as a bus kid growing up in central Illinois was the song "Read Your Bible, Pray Every Day." I liked the message of the song, but as a kid, I really liked the motions and actions. I remember singing the first verse, "Neglect your Bible, forget to pray, forget to pray, forget to pray; neglect your Bible, forget to pray and you'll shrink, shrink, shrink." I remember getting as low to the ground as possible, even lying flat on the ground. Then we would sing the second verse, "Read your Bible, pray every day, pray every day, pray every day; read your Bible, pray every day and you'll grow, grow, grow." I remember climbing up on my chair in Sunday School and getting as tall as I could just to show that I was "growing." I wonder if you are lying flat on your belly on the ground today because of your lack of reading God's Word, or are you as tall as possible due to your daily relationship with God's Word? Let's strive to believe that the Bible is the Word of God, and put our noses in it, and spend some time with God today. Books and other teaching tools are great, but nothing compares to the Word of God.

II Timothy 2:15–*"Study to shew thyself approved unto God, a workman that*

Not Just Your Mommy and Daddy's Religion

needeth not to be ashamed, rightly dividing the word of truth."

Joshua 1:8–*"This book of the law shall not depart out of thy mouth; but thou shalt meditate therein day and night, that thou mayest observe to do according to all that is written therein: for then thou shalt make thy way prosperous, and then thou shalt have good success."*

Psalm 1:2-3–*"But his delight is in the law of the LORD; and in his law doth he meditate day and night. And he shall be like a tree planted by the rivers of water, that bringeth forth his fruit in his season; his leaf also shall not wither; and whatsoever he doeth shall prosper."*

God has promised to bless us when we put ourselves in His Word. I am afraid many of us miss the blessings of God simply because we do not stay in the Word. Commit today to be a student of the Bible!

CHAPTER 2
THE AUTONOMY OF THE CHURCH
It Is Alive!

"I love going to church!" That's what my daughter said to me when she was just five years old. Church is a special place. Church is the place that God has commanded us to faithfully attend. I have heard preachers say that they had a "drug" problem as a teenager–not the drugs you are thinking of, but the fact that their parents

THE AUTONOMY OF THE CHURCH

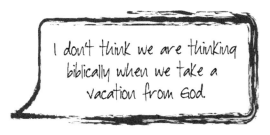

"drug" them to church every time the doors were open. As a young child, I rode the church bus to church every Sunday. Then for a while, my pastor, Norm Amstutz would drive by where we lived and pick up my brothers and me, and take us to church on Sunday and Wednesday evenings. Honestly, there were times I did not want to go, but my parents would send me anyway. Most of the time, however, I really enjoyed going to church. I had good friends at church, and I always knew the people there really loved me. My children have been in church literally since nine months before their birth; they have never had to wonder if we were going to attend church for every service–Missions Conference, Revival, any special function that would take place at our church. We are literally in church every service. Even when we go on vacation, we find a good Bible-believing church we can attend and are faithful to church. I don't believe we are thinking biblically when we take a vacation from God. Church is the gathering together of the local believers to worship God. Outside of personal devotions, church is the avenue for believers to learn more from the

Not Just Your Mommy and Daddy's Religion

Word of God on how we can serve and obey our Saviour.

I am the first to admit that there is no such thing as a perfect church. I have listened with great regret to some of the stories I have heard from people who used to attend church faithfully, but now will not attend because of some hurt or disappointment that another Christian caused in their life. The sad truth is that in the long run, the one that is really suffering because of that type of reaction is the one that has stopped attending church. The children that will grow up in a home where parents stopped attending church have so much less hope of growing in Christ. You are correct, there are no perfect churches. If there were a perfect church, it would cease from being perfect as soon as you or I joined it. Romans 3:23 is very clear, *"All have sinned."* Because I am a sinner, I will disappoint and hurt others around me. I am not making excuses for sinning; I am simply stating the facts. Before you cast judgment on me, however, the same is true for you as well. You think of the greatest Christian you know; they are still a sinner and will disappoint and hurt others. Don't ever allow someone else to control you to the point of disobeying God's clear command of being faithful to church. You determine now to be the parent that makes sure your family is faithful to obey God's command.

Some may say that they are the church. The Bible says in I Corinthians 6:19,

> *"What? know ye not that your body is the temple of the Holy Ghost which is in you, which ye have of God, and ye are not your own?"*

God literally dwells in us as believers, but that does not and should never take the place of attending church. The term *church* in the Bible literally means "a called out assembly." It is a local, visible group of believers that meet together regularly. Can you go out in the woods and meet with God? Yes! I do that often to spend time talking with my Saviour, but that cannot take the place of obeying God's command of being in the House of God faithfully.

Think about this: God believes in the church. In the Old Testament, the word *church* was not used, but God did establish the *tabernacle* and the *temple*. I am reminded of the children of Israel as they wandered in the wilderness; God had them make the tabernacle to worship Him. It was the people's responsibility to move that tabernacle with them everywhere they went. It was to be set up in the center of the camp for those millions of people. That is where they met with God. Don't get me wrong, I know we can meet with God anywhere anytime. You can even replace church attendance with livestream

Not Just Your Mommy and Daddy's Religion

services, but there is something special about being in the local church, hearing the preaching of the Word of God, and having the fellowship with other Christians. In the New Testament, we read of the birth of what we now call the *church*. Seventy-nine times God teaches us about the importance of the church.

IMPORTANCE OF THE CHURCH

You may ask, "Okay, but why do we go to church? What makes it so important?" I am glad you asked; I would love to tell you. First of all, God commands us to be faithful to church. Hebrews 10:25 says,

> *"Not forsaking the assembling of ourselves together, as the manner of some is; but exhorting one another: and so much the more, as ye see the day approaching."*

God literally commands every Christian to be faithful to the local church. As time goes by, our world gets more and more wicked.

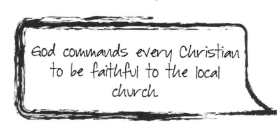

God commands every Christian to be faithful to the local church.

This ought to motivate every Christian to be more involved with church than ever before. This verse is probably one of the most used passages of Scripture regarding the importance of the local church, but that is not the only reference of the command of attending church faithfully. Take your Bible and study it. Acts 11:26 says,

> *"And when he had found him, he brought him unto Antioch. And it came to pass, that a whole year they assembled themselves with the church, and taught much people. And the disciples were called Christians first in Antioch."*

Also, I Corinthians 11:18 says,

> *"For first of all, when ye come together in the church."*

And look one more time back at Acts 14:27,

> *"And when they were come, and had gathered the church together, they rehearsed all that God had done with them, and how he had opened the door of faith unto the Gentiles."*

God places a great importance in being faithful to the local church. We are faithful to so many other things in our life like sporting events, school functions, even Sunday school socials, but we have a hard time being faithful to the church. Before we look deeper into the church, can I ask you some very pointed questions? How important is church to you? Are you okay with skipping services here and there? What are you willing to skip church for? Remember, Christ died for you. Christ loves you and desperately wants to spend time with you. Dedicate your life to always be faithful to the House of God.

FORMATION OF THE CHURCH

Not only is faithfulness to church commanded, but it is refreshing to know that the church was not made by some pastor, leadership team, or deacon board. God formed it and created it. I am sure every Christian would agree that if God made something for you and me to be involved with, that we should be faithful. God only created three organizations–the family, the church, and human government. God did not create the YMCA or a camping program; he put the importance on the local church. These other ministries are wonderful ministries and are very important, but they do not and should not take the place of or have authority over the local church. Please understand, as a youth pastor now for twenty-five years, I believe firmly in the ministry of summer camps. As a teen, I gave my summers to work at a summer camp ministry. My daughters have spent summers working at summer camp. If my pastor were to tell me that there is only one activity I could have for our youth ministry, you guessed it, it would be summer camp. I love summer camp! I believe it is the most important activity we have each year. But God died for the church, not the camp! My point is not to knock on other ministries, but to simply show you as a teenager how important the church is in God's eyes. I believe in the importance of the church. Let me challenge you to read the following passages of Scripture in relation to the importance of the local church: Matthew 16:18; Ephesians 5:23-27; I Corinthians 12:12-31.

LEADERSHIP OF THE CHURCH

Who is in charge of the Church? We obviously see the pastor behind the pulpit and automatically assume that he is the one in charge. Rather than me trying to rationalize or explain the leadership of the church, we can look in the Word of God to learn about the leadership of the local church. The leader and head of the church is and must be Jesus Christ. The Bible teaches in Ephesians 1:22,

> *"And hath put all things under his feet, and gave him to be the head over all things to the church."*

Not Just Your Mommy and Daddy's Religion

As well as in Ephesians 5:23 we read,

> *"For the husband is the head of the wife, even as Christ is the head of the church: and he is the saviour of the body."*

Also in Colossians 1:18 the Bible teaches,

> *"And he is the head of the body, the church: who is the beginning, the firstborn from the dead; that in all things he might have the preeminence."*

As you can easily see, the leader of the church is God Almighty, not a board, not a convention, not a group of elders or deacons.
God is the head of the church and we are to strive to please Him as our Leader.

This may come as a shock to you, but I have never seen God. I have, however, seen the work of God in the lives of people, but I have never seen Him.

> God always works through authority.

Also, I have never heard God's audible voice–I am sure it would scare me to death. One major principle that is vital in life and understanding God's Word is to understand that God always works through authority. I am a firm believer in following the authority God has placed in my life.

I preach regularly to teens the importance of following their authority which starts at home with Mom and Dad. However, God has placed other authority in your life as well. God established offices in the church to provide human leadership. That would be Biblical authority in all of our lives. I Corinthians 12:28 says,

> *"And God hath set some in the church, first apostles, secondarily prophets, thirdly teachers, after that miracles, then gifts of healings, helps, governments, diversities of tongues."*

The Bible teaches that leadership in the local church starts with the under-shepherd, or the pastor. We must learn to follow our pastor as the man that God has placed as the leader of the local church. I am not talking about pastor-worship. I love my pastor! I believe strongly that he is the man of God for my Church. I gladly and willingly follow his leadership. But at the same time, I know he is human. He makes mistakes and has failures in his life (please don't tell him I said that). It would be wrong for me to place him on a pedestal with Jesus Christ. Jesus Christ is the only perfect One who has walked on this earth. The way I am able to follow my pastor as

Not Just Your Mommy and Daddy's Religion

the leader of my church is by being a student of the Bible. I am required to personally study the Bible myself. I love to hear my pastor preach, but I am always interested in studying the Word of God myself as well. Your pastor has been placed in leadership of your church by God. Submit yourself to the authority of your pastor. Remember as well that God has placed some big qualifications on your pastor. I Timothy 3:1-7 is very specific. God sets the pastor in leadership, but requires a level of example and leadership from that man. God also placed leadership in the church in the form of deacons (literally translated as "servant leaders"). They are also required by God to follow a strict set of qualifications in order to fill the leadership position in the church (I Timothy 3:8-13). It is not my intention to over-emphasize or elevate the office of Pastor or deacon, but rather to reinforce the principle of authority in our life. God has placed authority in your life. I have often said that it is not my position to question the decisions of my pastor; it is my job to submit myself to his authority in my life. After all, I am not the pastor.

CHARGE TO THE CHURCH

Ultimately, we are here to follow through with the charge that God gave to the church. In the military, the commanding officer will require his subordinates to follow all of his orders. God has given the church (Christians) specific orders. God commands each of us to have a part in the "Great Commission."

We are all commanded to see people saved, to help them follow the Lord in baptism, and to help disciple or train them to follow Christ with their lives (Matthew 28:19-20). In other words, this is why the church is so important.

The church is designed to grow according to Acts 2:47,

> *"Praising God, and having favour with all the people. And the Lord added to the church daily such as should be saved."*

Just like you have grown through your elementary years now to your teen years to become the young man or young lady you are today, the church also must grow; otherwise it indicates that there is something severely wrong. The church has been given the charge from God to teach those who attend faithfully. Could you imagine attending a church where you never learned of the Gospel? Let me inform

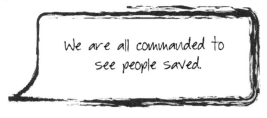

Not Just Your Mommy and Daddy's Religion

you, there are plenty of those types of churches in our world today. A church that does not teach the Gospel clearly is no more than a social group. There are enough social groups in our world today; we need churches that spend their time preaching and teaching the Word of God. Acts 20:28 teaches,

> *"Take heed therefore unto yourselves, and to all the flock, over the which the Holy Ghost hath made you overseers, to feed the church of God, which he hath purchased with his own blood."*

The church has also been ordered to care for the widows and fatherless according to James 1:27 which says,

> *"Pure religion and undefiled before God and the Father is this, To visit the fatherless and widows in their affliction, and to keep himself unspotted from the world."*

Let me just say it like my daughter said as a little five year-old child–I love my church! There is nothing like a local church that you can call home. A church where you would feel comfortable raising your own family someday. A church you would want your child finding a spouse in someday because you know the way he was taught and what he believes. I have had friends that attend other churches tell me in the past about the hesitations they have in their own church. Teen, it does not have to be that way for you. Plug into church. Jump in with both feet. When I get to visit other churches as I travel, even though I enjoy their services, I always look forward to getting home to my church. When I am away, I miss my church and the fellowship that I have with other Christians at my church. I support my church with my time and with my money. I defend my church when someone speaks ill against it, and I love being there every time the door is open, sometimes just going and opening the doors myself. Often, we are at the church very early, and most of the time we are the last to leave. I cannot get enough of church. How do you feel about your church? To make this chapter practical, can I encourage you to take the time to list out twenty-five things about your church that you thank God for? Also, list out the things you are doing right now to show your love and support for the church. Maybe that would involve ways you are serving the Lord in your church. I believe with all my heart that every teenager ought to serve in his church in some way. Find a job to do and get busy serving God in your local church this week. Let me encourage you to fall in love with your church!

I was reading through one of my wife's journals recently and found a paragraph on why the church is so important to every young man in

Not Just Your Mommy and Daddy's Religion

our world. The thought caught my attention because I figured it would also include the young ladies, but it did not. As I read in her journal, I found the following truth: Church is important to every young man because it is there you will find your W.I.F.E. The word wife was an acrostic for what the church provides for every believer:

Worship
Instruction
Fellowship and
Encouragement.

As true as this is, I also literally found my wife at church.

CHAPTER 3
THE PRIESTHOOD OF THE BELIEVERS
I'm Somebody to God

Let me tell you, this chapter contains one of my very favorite truths in all of the Word of God. It is my prayer that you read this entire chapter over and over again and really soak in the truths from the Bible relayed here. Please underline, highlight, and revisit these truths.

Have you ever been in a large group of people and felt so alone in the group because nobody even knew you were there–or at least that is how they treated you? There have been many times I have felt that way. I remember as a teenager attending my church youth ministry activities, and my youth pastor did not even know my name. He would often call me by the wrong name (in his defense, there were over one hundred teens). I remember thinking in my mind, even though my youth pastor did not know who I was, there is a God in Heaven that has billions and billions of people on earth, and He knows me personally.

Not only does God know me personally, but He also knows every detail of my life. He knows the very hairs of my head

> There is a God in Heaven that knows me personally.

and has them numbered–(Luke 12:7)–now that is amazing! God knows my thoughts and my desires. However, that is not just true about me; it is also true for you as well. With that in mind, God really longs to hear you talk directly to Him. It is this doctrine that separates us from some other religions of our day. We have the opportunity to

Not Just Your Mommy and Daddy's Religion

go directly to God ourselves. When you pray, you don't have to go to another man/priest in order to get word to God. You can go directly to God and approach His throne boldly through prayer (Hebrews 4:16). Take a moment to let that thought sink in–God Almighty, the Creator of the universe, the Sustainer of life, the Saviour of the world–wants to hear from you every day! WOW!

    I am a die-hard Chicago Cubs fan and have been since I was in kindergarten. I remember watching Cubs games with my grandma Hackney and cheering them on—on to another loss. They were the team with the longest championship drought in any professional sport. It was 108 years since they had last won the World Series. I am excited to report that the drought is now over. In 2016, they finally broke the "curse of the Billy goat" and won the World Series. However, prior to 2016, they were affectionately known as the "loveable losers." But I still loved that team. It has always been a dream of mine to meet some of the players. For my thirty-fifth birthday, my brother-in-law set it up for me to have lunch with the starting catcher for the Cubs. I remember how nervous I was, and yet how excited I was. That will go down as a highlight in my life to spend those three hours or so with Michael Barrett. The truth is though, he probably does not remember me, let alone my name, but God does! During the off-season before the 2016 baseball season, I had another great moment. I was able to take some teenage guys to a baseball clinic in Franklin, TN put on by a player by the name of Ben Zobrist. When we signed up to go to the clinic, Mr. Zobrist had finished the 2015 season by winning the World Series with the Kansas City Royals, and the week prior to our clinic, he signed a contract to play second base for the Cubbies! We spent a few hours with Mr. Zobrist that Saturday afternoon as he told those teen guys how to play baseball, but more importantly about the love of Jesus for them and their need to trust in Jesus Christ as their personal Saviour. What a day that was! But again, I am quite sure that Mr. Zobrist wouldn't recognize me if he saw me and certainly would not know my name. But Jesus does!

No matter how lonely or alone you may feel, there is a God in Heaven that knows you and longs to spend valuable time with you every day!

The Bible lists out numerous verses that teach this truth–you can go directly to God yourself. He hears you and cares about what you are saying! I am reminded of just a small amount of the mass of verses that teach this principle clearly. The Bible teaches in Exodus 19:6,

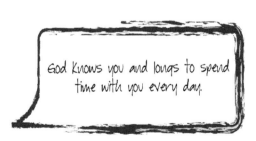
God knows you and longs to spend time with you every day.

Not Just Your Mommy and Daddy's Religion

> *"And ye shall be unto me a kingdom of priests, and an holy nation."*

Also Isaiah 61:6 teaches,

> *"But ye shall be named the Priests of the LORD: men shall call you the Ministers of our God."*

I Peter 2:5 says,

> *"Ye also, as lively stones, are built up a spiritual house, an holy priesthood, to offer up spiritual sacrifices, acceptable to God by Jesus Christ."*

Revelation 1:6 says,

> *"And hath made us kings and priests unto God and his Father; to him be glory and dominion for ever and ever. Amen."*

As you can easily see, God loves you and longs to hear from you directly.

One of my favorite verses in all the Bible (I have a lot of them) is found in Matthew 11:28 which says,

> *"Come unto me, all ye that labour and are heavy laden, and I will give you rest."*

It does not matter what you are facing today. Your troubles are not too big for God. You have the ability as a Christian teenager to go directly to God with whatever issue you are facing. You do not have to wait to build a relationship with God until you are an adult. Let's make it personal and practical. That test or exam you are facing, God already knows the tension you feel and is there to help you and cares about the outcome. In my mind, I take great comfort in that thought because God already knows all the answers to that test anyway. He really wants to help you! The issues you are facing at home where it seems like mom and dad are always fighting and may get a divorce, the financial struggles your family faces, even the prayer requests about the private things in your life– God knows and cares. Guys, God even knows about the girl you really like and are not willing to tell anyone else about. God knows about you in every way and still loves you and wants to build that relationship with you. I am afraid that we don't go to Him like we should. It seems that the only time we get really serious about our prayer life is when there is trouble. Don't get me wrong, God does want to help us when we face the troubles in our life, but He also wants to hear from us when things are going great, and we just want to spend time bragging on Him and praising Him.

Not Just Your Mommy and Daddy's Religion

What I learn from the doctrine of the Priesthood of the Believers is that I am important to God. Yes, God loves your preacher and youth pastor, but you are just as important to Him as those preachers and teachers you have. There are NO "big-wigs" in God's family. I have two daughters, and I love them more than words could ever express. I love to spend time with them and play games. I never dreamed that I would ever play with American Girl dolls or Polly Pockets, but just to spend time with those girls was worth it to me. I can assure you that we did that many years ago when my girls were little, but to be honest, I would do it again if they were to ask me. No, I

> There are NO "big-wigs" in God's family.

did not do it in public, but if it meant I got to spend more time with my girls, I will do more than I ever dreamed I would. Teenager, God loves you a ton more than I could ever love my girls. God longs to have special time with you. I am afraid all too often though, we neglect God. Outside of praying for the meal with your family, when was the last time you got alone with God just to tell Him how much you love Him? When I was a kid, I jokingly prayed the following prayer, even though I cannot tell you where I learned the prayer, but I remember it clearly:

> "Now I lay me down to rest,
> A pile of books upon my chest.
> If I should die before I wake,
> That's one less test I'll have to take."

As true as that prayer is, it was not one of those prayers that helped grow my relationship with Christ. I'm talking about spending time with God like you would with your best friend.

I remember as a teenager, my youth pastor, David Bush, challenged me to spend time praying every chance I could get. I decided to follow his advice. I remember driving down the road talking to God as if He were sitting in the passenger seat with me. Of course riding with me, He certainly had to wear His seatbelt. I remember working a job my junior and senior years cleaning office buildings. As I was vacuuming the doctor's office floor, I would pray out loud. This always took place after hours late at night or even early in the morning, but on occasion the doctor would walk in and hear me talking out loud to God–that was a little embarrassing–but he was a Christian too, so he understood. What I am saying is spend time with God! We make plenty of time to talk to others on the phone, texts, emails, or social media, but God usually gets left out. Let's band together and encourage one another to spend some time with God every day.

Not Just Your Mommy and Daddy's Religion

Wait, you are not just speaking to the air; you are speaking to a God that hears and answers your prayers. I am reminded of the saying "prayer changes things!" Here is a list of verses that you need to look up and put to memory: James 5:12, I Timothy 2:8, I Thessalonians 5:17, Colossians 4:2, Philippians 14:6, Ephesians 6:18, John 16:24, Luke 21:36, Luke 18:1, Matthew 26:41, Matthew 7:7 and I Chronicles 16:11. All of these verses deal with the fact that God hears what you have to say and will answer your prayers according to His will. All of this has one major factor involved: it all revolves around you. You must go to God! He is not going to force you to spend time with Him. He simply wants you to love Him and spend time with Him. As a Christian, you can go directly to Him in prayer.

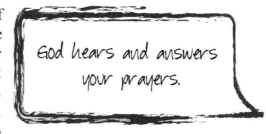
God hears and answers your prayers.

Let me give you some tips to help develop your walk with Christ. First, make a prayer list. You can write it in a journal, or just keep a piece of paper in your Bible. I keep my prayer list on my phone so that it is with me everywhere I go. Second, try to locate a special place to pray. It may be in your bedroom or some place private. My wife literally has a closet that she uses every day as her prayer room. She calls it her "war room." She goes to that special place every day. It is not the only place to go pray, but it is her special place to get alone with her Lord. Can I encourage you to get a special place that you go to physically be alone with Christ? Make that your place of prayer. Third, schedule a specific time to pray every day. Make an appointment with God every day. Life is so busy. It is easy to neglect something like prayer because we are wrapped up in a school project, or a ball team, or even sitting down with the family to watch a program. There are always things that will clamor for your time, and if we are not careful, our prayer life is the first thing to go. Schedule that time every day. Put a reminder in your phone. Don't neglect that prayer time. Last, I would encourage you to pray out loud. I know, if someone is listening, they may think you are losing your mind. Although that may be true too, I have found that when I pray out loud, I stay more focused on what I am praying about. Talk to God as if He were right there with you (over time you will come to realize He really is right there with you). Because Jesus loves you so much, He seeks to spend time with you. Don't leave a relationship with God just to the adults. You can have that close relationship with Him even now as a teenager. Start today!

CHAPTER 4
THE TWO ORDINANCES
My Obedience is Important

My goal with this chapter is to be very helpful and practical. I could get really deep into the theological teachings of the ordinances of the local church, but I will attempt to make this chapter informative and simple. It is my desire that you are able to take truths from this chapter to apply to your life today in simple and practical ways. I remember being taught by my pastor to keep things simple. Don't over-complicate your subject. Let's start with the basics. I checked with Webster's Dictionary to find out the definition of the word *ordinance*. Webster defined *ordinance* as:

1. An authoritative decree or direction
2. Something ordained or decreed by fate or deity
3. A prescribed usage, practical or ceremonial

The Bible teaches us there are only two ordinances given to the local church: observing the Lord's Supper and the Baptism of converts. We will cover each of these ordinances separately. Both are important and are the job of the local church as commanded by God.

BAPTISM

I remember when my daughters were younger; when we would have the occasion of going swimming, they would ask me to baptize them in the pool just for fun. We would practice often, and it was a lot of fun for both of them as well as for me. What keeps that practice of a baptism from being performed by just anyone in their

Not Just Your Mommy and Daddy's Religion

own home swimming pool or bathtub? Why can't the neighbor down the street hold a neighborhood baptismal service? The biblical reason is that the ordinance was given to the local church and not to the people practicing in the pool for neighborhood dunking day.

The Bible says in Acts 2:41,

> *"Then they that gladly received his word were baptized: and the same day there were added unto them about three thousand souls."*

The word *Baptism* in Greek literally means to "dip under." There are some guidelines that must be followed in the matter of baptism. Please don't zone out during all the details, I promise to get very practical shortly to you as a teenager. In Acts 8:36-38 we learn from the Ethiopian eunuch that the first requirement to be baptized is that the matter of salvation by simple faith and trust in Christ has **already** taken place. This separates us from some other false religious teachings that instruct that baptism is a part of salvation. Some teach that if you are not baptized, you are not truly saved and therefore will spend eternity in Hell. Acts 8:37 says,

> *"And Philip said, If thou believest with all thine heart, thou mayest. And he answered and said, I believe that Jesus Christ is the Son of God."*

THE TWO ORDINANCES

Acts 16:30-34 says,

> *"And brought them out, and said, Sirs, what must I do to be saved? And they said, Believe on the Lord Jesus Christ, and thou shalt be saved, and thy house. And they spake unto him the word of the Lord, and to all that were in his house. And he took them the same hour of the night, and washed their stripes; and was baptized, he and all his, straightway. And when he had brought them into his house, he set meat before them, and rejoiced, believing in God with all his house."*

It is so important to understand that the baptism of the believer is just that–for the believer. As Baptists, we firmly believe that baptism is important. After all, we are called Baptists. However, we believe the Bible teaches plainly that baptism is an action that takes place following conversion. Some will teach in error that baptism is a necessary part of salvation. I ask you simply about the thief on the cross that died beside Jesus. If you remember, the Bible says in Matthew 27:44 that both of the thieves that were crucified with Christ railed on Jesus, and even said if He truly was the Son of God that he should save Himself and them next to Him. However, within a short amount of time, one of those thieves changed his thoughts about Jesus and actually asked Jesus to remember him when He went to His Kingdom. Jesus replied by saying in Luke 23:43 *"And Jesus said unto him, Verily I say unto thee, To day shalt thou be with me in paradise."* That one thief was converted and was saved. Now, it was impossible for him to be baptized since he was already hanging on the cross. If baptism were a part of salvation, how can that thief be saved since he was never baptized? Also, think about this; if baptism is part of Salvation, then I ask you why did Jesus Himself not baptize?

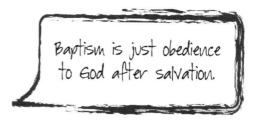

John 4:2 clearly says Jesus did not baptize. We know He came into this world to *"seek and to save that which was lost."* (Luke 19:10). In the Romans Road to salvation there is no mention of baptism. John 3:16 does not mention baptism. My point is simple–baptism is not a part of salvation; it is just obedience to God following salvation.

THE METHOD OF BAPTISM

The method of baptism taught in the Word of God is by immersion–being placed under the water and being brought back up again. Baptism is a beautiful picture of the death, burial, and resurrection of Jesus Christ. When I baptize someone, I say out loud, "Buried in baptism, raised to walk in newness of life." Our baptism pictures the change that has already taken place in our hearts because of our conversion. There are some religions that practice baptism by sprinkling, but even by definition and example in the Bible, baptism is practiced by immersion, going under the water. I know some would even ask if that really matters. The simple answer is yes. You will only find the example of Baptism in the Bible when the person goes under the water and back up again. I want to teach our teens the importance of following the Bible. The Bible gives the example of baptism even in Jesus' life in passages like Mark 1:9-11,

> *"And it came to pass in those days, that Jesus came from Nazareth of Galilee, and was baptized of John in Jordan. And straightway coming up out of the water, he saw the heavens opened, and the Spirit like a dove descending upon him: And there came a voice from heaven, saying, Thou art my beloved Son, in whom I am well pleased."*

Look at Acts 8:38, it says,

Not Just Your Mommy and Daddy's Religion

"And he commanded the chariot to stand still: and they went down both into the water, both Philip and the eunuch; and he baptized him."

Okay, let's get practical; have you followed the Lord in believer's baptism? Are you living in obedience to the command of the Lord in this area of baptism? An illustration to help explain baptism is that of the wedding ring. I was married on January 1, 1994. On that day, my wife placed on my left hand, a wedding ring. That ring pictures something that is true in my life–I am a married man. However, if I don't wear that wedding ring, am I still married? Of course I am. That ring has a purpose of telling the world that I belong to Christy Copeland. Baptism is to the Christian what the ring is to my marriage. It is a picture of something that has happened already in my life. There are Christians today that are saved and have not been baptized. Can I encourage you to go ahead and obey Christ and "put on the ring?" If you are saved and have not yet been baptized, you are not living in obedience to God and His Word.

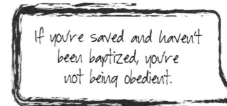

If you're saved and haven't been baptized, you're not being obedient.

God commands you to get this taken care of. So why are you waiting? Jesus Christ even gave us His personal example of getting baptized. Let me challenge you to follow His example. Talk to your pastor or youth pastor today, and let's get that taken care of this Sunday!

LORD'S SUPPER

The second ordinance that the church is commanded to administer is the Lord's Supper. Some would call it communion. The Lord's Supper was established for the purpose of remembering what Christ did for us in His suffering on the cross in our place. It was pictured in the Old Testament with the Passover which looked forward to the Messiah coming. Also, we see in the New Testament in I Corinthians that the early church practiced the Lord's Supper. It has been practiced down through the ages as an opportunity for Christians to look back at what Christ did for us as He gave His life on the cross for each of us. Some churches observe this ordinance in different ways. Some practice "closed communion" which means you must be a saved, baptized, and a member of that local church in order to participate in the Lord's Supper. Others practice "open communion" which means you only must be a professing Christian that has been baptized. Membership in any particular church is not necessary. A third way churches observe the

Not Just Your Mommy and Daddy's Religion

Lord's Supper is called "close communion" which means that you would need to be saved, baptized, and a member of a church of like faith and practice of the church that you are observing the Lord's Supper. How often should you take the Lord's Supper? You may be part of a church that observes the Lord's Supper every month or every other month. What is the frequency with which we are to observe the Lord's Supper? Acts 2:46 says,

> *"And they, continuing daily with one accord in the temple, and breaking bread from house to house, did eat their meat with gladness and singleness of heart,"*

which means that they did it every time they met together. Acts 20:7 says,

> *"And upon the first day of the week, when the disciples came together to break bread, Paul preached unto them, ready to depart on the morrow; and continued his speech until midnight."*

This verse indicates they observed the Lord's Supper on a weekly basis. I Corinthians 11:26 teaches,

> *"For as often as ye eat this bread, and drink this cup, ye do shew the Lord's death till he come."*

This verse just says as *"as often as ye."* The frequency that your church observes the Lord's Supper is totally up to your pastor.

THE PURPOSE OF THE LORD'S SUPPER

The purpose of the Lord's Supper is simply for us to not take for granted what Jesus Christ did for us on the cross. We would be on our way to Hell today, but for the great sacrifice that Christ made for us on the cross. A number of years ago, my daughters begged me to build them a playhouse in our backyard. I know as a child I always wanted a fort of my own, and my daughters really wanted that special playhouse. My wife helped me decide what to build. I wanted to make it extra special for my girls; after all, they would never forget what I built for them. We went online and actually purchased some blueprints for the build. I got busy working on that special playhouse nearly every Monday and Tuesday evening, as well as basically all day each Saturday. It took me two months to complete the project. I shot my hand with a framing nail gun in the process. But when it was done, wow, it was amazing! It has a front porch, a main floor, a ladder on the wall that leads to the loft, and to top it off, I added a third level with a slide leading from level three down to

Not Just Your Mommy and Daddy's Religion

level two. My daughters loved it! They worked with their mom to decorate that playhouse inside and out. I added electricity so that they had plugs and lights. It is basically a miniature house even with air conditioning. My daughters would spend hours out there playing. They would invite friends over and they would sleep outside in the playhouse overnight. Really, it was an amazing place. However, I cannot tell you the last time my daughters have gone out to the playhouse. When we have the teens from the church over to the house, they always go to the playhouse just to have a blast. My point is many times we get used to the things we have and the blessings we enjoy. We all do that. It could be a game system you had to have, but now the newness has worn off. It may be that swimming pool your parents had put in just for you, now it is "Old Hat." What about the pet you begged your parents for and now it is just a chore feeding and bathing that animal. We simply take for granted the things we have been blessed with.

God gives a stern warning in the Bible regarding the Lord's Supper. The Bible says in I Corinthians 11:27-28,

> "Wherefore whosoever shall eat this bread, and drink this cup of the Lord, unworthily, shall be guilty of the body and blood of the Lord. But let a man

THE TWO ORDINANCES

examine himself, and so let him eat of that bread, and drink of that cup."

Unworthily means that we take the Lord's Supper with sin in our life. Make the Lord's Supper personal. For me, the Lord's Supper is one more chance to look at what Jesus did for me and to realize I should and could be doing more for him. I search my heart and do some "house cleaning."

There are churches that teach that the bread and grape juice actually become the body and blood of Jesus. The term that describes this belief is called *transubstantiation*. Let me tell you that Jesus only died once for us, not every time we observe the Lord's Supper. Just like the baptism, the Lord's Supper is commanded 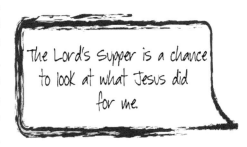 to be observed by every Christian in the local church. Make both of these ordinances something special in your life. I love the fact that by taking the Lord's Supper, I am worshiping Christ and honoring Him by meditating on what He did for me by dying on the cross to provide for my Salvation. Don't take for granted what Jesus did for you. Don't look at these ordinances the same as you did before learning these principles in your life.

Not Just Your Mommy and Daddy's Religion

I remember as a teenager sitting on the second row of my church during the Lord's Supper. When I was a teenager, my pastor was Dr. Bob Kelley. I would watch him during the Lord's Supper, and I saw how important it was to him. Behind him on our back wall was a stain glass window with a cross in it (which is still there today). I still remember having tears come down my face as I looked at that cross on the stain glass window and I pictured in my mind what Jesus did for me on the cross of Calvary. Let it be a special time that helps you draw closer to the Saviour.

What does all this mean to you today, teenager? How is this practical? Are you today obedient to God in the first ordinance of baptism? Have you followed the Lord in believer's baptism? If not, can I encourage you to get that taken care of this Sunday? And second, when your church observes the Lord's Supper, how seriously do you participate? Is it a time of looking into your own heart and making sure things are right with your Saviour? It can be a time of great closeness with Christ, thanking Him for what He has done to provide for you eternal life. We are Baptists–this is what we believe.

CHAPTER 5
INDIVIDUAL SOUL LIBERTY
We All Will Answer For Ourselves

Don't let the title scare you. That just simply means that you will give an account of yourself to God someday. In our society today, we have learned that we can do whatever we want and simply blame it on someone else. It seems that people get away with whatever they want if they can simply blame their actions on someone else. However, you will not be able to blame someone else for why you did or did not serve God to the best of your ability. God knows all (omniscient) and God sees all (omnipresent). The Bible says in Romans 14:12,

> *"So then every one of us shall give account of himself to God."*

The Bible is clear that there is a judgment that we will all face someday. Hebrews 9:27 clearly states,

> *"And as it is appointed unto men once to die, but after this the judgment."*

Both Christians and unbelievers will face judgment. The Bible teaches of two great judgments that will take place someday soon.

THE GREAT WHITE THRONE JUDGMENT

There is a judgment for the unbelievers called the Great White Throne Judgment. This judgment is designed only for those who have not placed their faith and trust in Jesus Christ as their personal Saviour. As a Christian, you will not face this judgment. At this judgment, the unsaved people will face God Almighty, and will be found guilty of their sin, and will be cast into the Lake of Fire for all eternity. This judgment is not to determine if someone will enter into Heaven or not. This is only for those that have not trusted Christ. People will plead for God's mercy based on their good works, but to no avail. Matthew 7:22 says,

> *"Many will say to me in that day, Lord, Lord, have we not prophesied in thy name? and in thy name have cast out devils? and in thy name done many wonderful works? And then will I profess unto them, I never knew you: depart from me, ye that work iniquity."*

I cannot imagine the tears that will be shed on this horrific day when we as Christians witness this terrible judgment on the unsaved world. The Great White Throne Judgment will take place at the end of the thousand year reign of Christ, which is called the Millennium. Christian, take comfort, you will not face God's judgment there, but your family might face that judgment if they are unsaved. The Great White

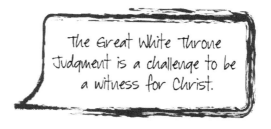

The Great White Throne Judgment is a challenge to be a witness for Christ.

Throne Judgment is a tremendous challenge to me to be a witness for Christ more and more. I don't want anyone to face this horrific judgment.

I think regularly about my aunts and uncles, my cousins, my distant family, as well as my neighbors and the scores of people that I have contact with each day. Are they on their way to Heaven, or will they be cast into the Lake of Fire someday? I must be faithful in telling everyone I can about the Love of Christ and how He wants them in Heaven with Him someday. Let me ask you directly, what are you doing to help keep people out of Hell? Revelation 20:12 says,

> *"And I saw the dead, small and great, stand before God; and the books were opened: and another book was opened, which is the book of life: and the dead were judged out of those things which were written in the books, according to their works."*

This judgment is real; people will spend all eternity in the Lake of Fire who are judged here at this judgment. Take a minute and seriously think about your loved one being cast into the Lake of Fire and turning back to you and asking you, "Why didn't you warn me?" What a tremendous burden to bear, but yet what a great opportunity for us now. Christ has not returned yet; there is still time to warn the lost world. Can

Not Just Your Mommy and Daddy's Religion

I challenge you to make a private list of those you need to tell about Christ? Begin today to pray every day for them by name. As the Lord gives you opportunity, share with them about the love of Christ. Remember, God's Word says in II Peter 3:9,

> *"The Lord is not slack concerning his promise, as some men count slackness; but is longsuffering to us-ward, not willing that any should perish, but that all should come to repentance."*

God wants to see that person saved that you are thinking of right now. He just needs a willing servant to go and tell them! Will you be the one?

THE JUDGMENT SEAT OF CHRIST

As a Christian, there is a different judgment that you and I will face someday. It is called the Judgment Seat of Christ, or also called the Bema Seat Judgment. II Corinthians 5:10 says,

> *"For we must all appear before the judgment seat of Christ; that every one may receive the things done in his body, according to that he hath done, whether it be good or bad."*

This judgment is designed for Christians only. There will be absolutely no unsaved people present at The Judgment Seat of Christ. This judgment will take place following the Rapture of the Church. The trumpet will sound and we will be raptured to meet Christ in the air. This event will also start the seven years of Tribulation here on the earth. It is a comforting thought that we as Christians will not be on the earth at all during the Great Tribulation. We will not be present during all the chaos here on earth. We will be with Jesus in Heaven. The Rapture of the Church is the event that takes place directly before the Judgment Seat of Christ. It is at this judgment that we will all give an account of ourselves to Christ. We sometimes have a wrong perception of this judgment. I remember as a child hearing preaching on this Judgment as the preacher painted a picture of God dropping a screen and showing all the bad things I had ever done in my life for everyone to see. Oh, the fear that struck my heart thinking of the embarrassment that I was sure to face! Many times this judgment is taught as a negative time. And although there is an aspect of this judgment that can be negative, I believe the Bible teaches there is also a very positive aspect of the Judgment Seat of Christ. Revelation 22:16 says,

> *"And, behold, I come quickly; and my reward is with me, to give every man according as his work shall be."*

Notice God is bringing His rewards with Him! There is a reward that God wants to bring to each Christian. Remember, every person at this judgment will spend all eternity in Heaven with Christ. This is not a judgment on the sins that we have committed; God has already forgiven us of our sins. John 5:24 is still in the Bible and says,

> *"Verily, verily, I say unto you, He that heareth my word, and believeth on him that sent me, hath everlasting life, and shall not come into condemnation; but is passed from death unto life."*

Did you hear that verse? You will *"not come into condemnation;"* Couple that verse with Hebrews 10:17 which says,

> *"And their sins and iniquities will I remember no more."*

My sin is GONE! Psalm 103:12 says,

> *"As far as the east is from the west, so far hath he removed our transgressions from us."*

God says He will never remember it again! Micah 7:19 agrees by saying,

> *"He will turn again, he will have compassion upon us; he will subdue our iniquities; and thou wilt cast all their sins into the depths of the sea."*

It is about right now where I have a hard time sitting down typing this book! To think that Jesus died on the cross to pay ALL my sin debt, and that at salvation, Jesus Christ forgave me of all my sins, never to be remembered again; how can I not serve Him with all my heart? Praise the Lord for this great doctrine! I remember singing the song in Children's Church about my sins being forgiven. I am not a very good singer, but I sure love to sing this song. My sins are G-O-N-E gone! One of my goals in this book is that teenagers would learn to study the Word of God for themselves. Don't fret over the giant video screen in front of all the other Christians in Heaven. After studying my Bible, I have found that teaching not to be accurate. It does make for motivational preaching, but it is not true to the Word of God. However, on the positive side, the Bible teaches that at this judgment, God is looking to hand out rewards and crowns to those who have served Him during their earthly life.

The Greek word used in the Bible referring to the Judgment seat of Christ is the word *"Bema."*

The word literally means "judgment seat" and refers to a "reward seat" but not to a judicial bench. This is not a picture of a court room with a judge getting ready to pronounce judgment on a guilty person. Rather, it is a picture of rewards getting ready to be handed out to participants in a race or competition. I believe it is similar to the award ceremony of the Olympics. Picture the competition coming to a completion as the contestants compete to the end.

All participate with great fervor and passion, but the awards are only given to the three best. Bronze, silver, and gold medallions are awarded to the three best contestants. The remainder of the contestants all "suffer loss" only because rewards were held back from them. Today, a great host of witnesses are cheering us on as Christians.

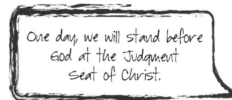
One day, we will stand before God at the Judgment Seat of Christ.

They want each of us to win the prize or the reward that Christ has waiting for us. What a great picture of what will take place some day in Heaven. One day, we will stand before God at this Judgment Seat of Christ to receive the crowns and rewards that are due us for our life that we have lived here on this earth for Christ. This ceremony will not take place for an occasion of pride or arrogance, but rather so that we can honor and worship Christ as we cast those crowns back at His feet as we learn from Revelation 4:10-11,

> *"The four and twenty elders fall down before him that sat on the throne, and worship him that liveth for ever and ever, and cast their crowns before the throne, saying, Thou art worthy, O Lord, to receive glory and honour and power: for thou hast created all things, and for thy pleasure they are and were created."*

I am motivated to serve Him more and more! I do not want to stand before God empty-handed one day. I don't work for Christ so that I can earn a spot in Heaven. My mansion in Heaven is already mine based upon my faith in what Christ did for me on the cross. However, I am motivated to serve Him to the best of my ability because of the Salvation He has provided for me. I want to challenge you to look up and study these other verses concerning the Judgment Seat of Christ: Romans 14:10; Revelation 22:12; II Corinthians 5:10; and I Corinthians 3:10-15.

THE CHOICE

With that positive view of the Judgment Seat of Christ in mind, I do want to caution you about the possible negative aspect of the Judgment Seat of Christ. In our society today, we are taught to blame others for the problems in our life. We hear about kids blaming parents for problems in their lives. We see teens blaming teachers for their problems in school. We see adults blaming their bosses or their childhood issues for their bad behavior of today. This has been a problem since the beginning of time in the Garden of Eden when Adam said to God in Genesis 3:12,

> *"The woman whom thou gavest to be with me, she gave me of the tree, and I did eat."*

Teenager, one day you will not be able to tell God you would have done more for Him if it were not for your parents or some other authority. If you fail to serve God to the best of your potential, there will be nobody else to blame. It will be totally and completely your choice. Romans 14:10 says,

> *"But why dost thou judge thy brother? or why dost thou set at nought thy brother? for we shall all stand before the judgment seat of Christ."*

You will stand before God one day alone! There will be those at the Judgment Seat of Christ who suffer loss as they stand before Christ. I Corinthians 3:10-15 says,

"According to the grace of God which is given unto me, as a wise masterbuilder, I have laid the foundation, and another buildeth thereon. But let every man take heed how he buildeth thereupon. For other foundation can no man lay than that is laid, which is Jesus Christ. Now if any man build upon this foundation gold, silver, precious stones, wood, hay, stubble; Every man's work shall be made manifest: for the day shall declare it, because it shall be revealed by fire; and the fire shall try every man's work of what sort it is. If any man's work abide which he hath built thereupon, he shall receive a reward. If any man's work shall be burned, he shall suffer loss: but he himself shall be saved; yet so as by fire."

This powerful passage of Scripture teaches us that we could suffer the loss of some reward that we could have received if only we would have done more for the One who died on the cross for us. Some would say that this has to do with our motives behind what we do for Christ while here on earth. Others would say it is because of the works that we did not accomplish because we were not in the perfect will of God. I believe both aspects are true. My point is, you don't have to suffer loss, you can receive many crowns and rewards as you stand before your Creator

Not Just Your Mommy and Daddy's Religion

because of the way you lived for Him here on earth. The Bible teaches of at least five specific crowns that will be given at this judgment:

1. An incorruptible crown—I Corinthians 9:25
2. A crown of rejoicing—I Thessalonians 2:19
3. A crown of righteousness—I Timothy 4:8
4. A crown of life—James 1:12
5. A grown of glory—I Peter 5:4

Which crowns are you going to be given by the nail-pierced hands of Jesus?

Let me ask you teenager, at which judgment will you be judged? This is totally and specifically up to you. God will not decide which judgment you will attend. If you have not trusted Jesus Christ as your Saviour, do so right now. He wants to save you. However, as a Christian, you will be at the Judgment Seat of Christ getting ready to enter Heaven. While you are still here in this life, are you helping to keep others from the Great White Throne Judgment? You have the opportunity to see souls around you saved even today. Strive today to see someone trust Christ. With God's help we can reach our world for Christ and keep people from the eternal Lake of Fire. Along the way then, we are serving Christ and laying up treasure in Heaven. Either way, we all will stand before Jesus someday in judgment.

CHAPTER 6
SEPARATION
Let People Know Who You Are

As I discussed early in this text, I am a Chicago Cubs fan! It does not take long for someone to be around me to know who my favorite baseball team is. I remember cheering on the Cubs as far back as five years old. It was my desire to see the Cubs win a World Series someday. Of course that has been the desire of Cubs fans for over the

SEPARATION

last 108 years–until 2016! I show I am a Cubs fan when I wear Cubs hats and shirts; I even have a Cubs tool belt, vanity plates, and all sorts of memorabilia. I can recite stats and talk all day about the players that have played and currently play for the Chicago Cubs. There is no doubt to anyone that I am a Cubs fan!

We have no problem supporting our favorite sports teams or hobbies, but I would be a poor Christian if I let people know about my love for a secular ball club and not let them know about my love for the Saviour of my soul. You see; I was a lost sinner on my way to a Devil's Hell, but Jesus rescued me. How could I ever be ashamed of the One who died for me? I am not afraid to let the whole world know I am a Christian. I have heard it said by atheists that if we as Christians really believed that Hell was really real, how could we keep from proclaiming the love of Christ all over the world in order to keep people out of Hell? I guess the truth is that either we really don't believe what the Bible says, or we are just simply ashamed to be called Christians. It was Paul who said in Romans 1:16,

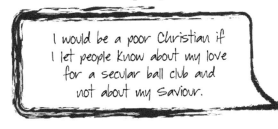
I would be a poor Christian if I let people know about my love for a secular ball club and not about my Saviour.

Not Just Your Mommy and Daddy's Religion

"For I am not ashamed of the gospel of Christ: for it is the power of God unto salvation to every one that believeth; to the Jew first, and also to the Greek."

Even Paul had to come to the point in his life that he was more concerned about what God thought than what man thought. I was in our Sunday morning teen church a few years back, and I saw one of our bus teens wearing one of those "Christian T- Shirts." Typically I admire a teen that is willing to put Jesus's name on their clothes and wear them publically. This particular shirt said "Undercover Christian." At first glance, I really liked the shirt the teen was wearing, but as I thought more about the message of the shirt, I was taken back. In my mind I thought it was sad because truly that is the way that most teenagers live their Christian lives. Don't be an undercover Christian; let everyone know Whom you belong to. I have also seen the shirts that say "PROPERTY OF . . ." It wasn't but a few weeks later that another teen was wearing a shirt that said "PROPERTY OF GOD!" Wouldn't it be great if every teenager had the heart that said publically to everybody that, "I BELONG TO GOD!" Don't be ashamed of Christ.

ECCLESIASTICAL SEPARATION

There are two aspects of separation that we as Baptists believe. First, there is the matter of Ecclesiastical Separation. Don't let that big word scare you; it just simply means church separation. I heard a preacher say a very profound statement in a sermon, he said, "Things that are different are not the same." I know, you are thinking that is an obvious statement, and you are right. Things that are different are not the same. The college I went to is different from the college God may have chosen for you to go to someday–that is okay. The high school I attended is probably different from the one that you attend as well. The problem comes when someone says, "I go to such and such a denomination church, and they teach the same thing that you Baptists teach there at your church." Be careful teenager! There are different kinds of churches in our world today because there are different kinds of doctrines (teachings) being taught. If they say they attend a Church of Christ, then they teach different things about the matter of salvation and eternal security than you are learning in your Baptist church. If they are Catholic, then they teach different doctrine in the matter of Jesus Christ and your accessibility to pray to God the Father. My point is that things that are different are not the same when it comes to churches.

Not Just Your Mommy and Daddy's Religion

I am an Independent Baptist youth pastor. I am an Independent Baptist not just by choice, but by conviction in the teachings from the Word of God. I am not being critical of other people, but I am saying that I would not and could not follow the teachings of those different denominations. That is why I cannot have a youth fellowship with a church that does not teach the doctrine of the Baptist church. I do not want to, and biblically cannot, team up with or "yolk up" with someone who would teach my teenagers that they could lose their salvation, when the Word of God is very clear in this matter. I will, and I do, have great fellowship with other churches of like faith and practice. That means; if the church preaches the Bible and practices what is taught in the Bible, I can, and do, have fellowship with that church and youth ministry. However, there is never a reason to be hateful or mean-spirited about the matter of separation. That has never been taught by God nor demonstrated by Christ. An Independent Baptist should not have a hateful, critical spirit. We have a responsibility to stand tall for Christ, but in a loving and compassionate way. Jesus is the perfect example of having a compassion for those around Him. I

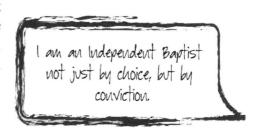

I am an Independent Baptist not just by choice, but by conviction.

want to encourage you teenager, look at your church and know why you attend your church. Know what your church believes and the biblical reason behind what your church believes. Ask God for His wisdom and discernment to see the error in other churches and the strength never to go backwards in your church separation. It seems the longer I am serving with teenagers; I am more and more burdened about this particular area. Our churches are changing drastically year after year. It seems as though it is hard to find a church that will still hold to the Biblical values we have learned. Many churches today resemble more of a social club than that of a church. I have made it my passion to teach our teens that our youth services are church services. I want our teens to love church because of hearing the preaching of God's Word, not just the fellowship they have with each other. I want our teens to learn to sing scriptural songs that bring honor and glory to Jesus Christ, not the type that feed the flesh. What type of church will your kids have someday if our society continues to tell us what church needs to be like? I am here to say that it will not resemble church much at all. It is important to protect the church. Don't let the world change the church.

Not Just Your Mommy and Daddy's Religion

PERSONAL SEPARATION

Okay, now this particular topic is one that tends to be very divisive, and, if not handled in the right way, stirs up resentful feelings in some people. However, this is a vital Baptist Distinctive that is quickly shunned by many. Can I ask you to read with an open mind to the Spirit of God in your life? This is an important aspect of separation that must be discussed—that is the matter of personal separation. I Peter 2:9 says,

> *"But ye are a chosen generation, a royal priesthood, an holy nation, a peculiar people; that ye should shew forth the praises of him who hath called you out of darkness into his marvellous light."*

God says, as Christians we are a peculiar people. That does not mean you have to walk around as "Billy Bible" or "Sally Spiritual." The term *peculiar people* literally means "purchased," or "acquired," God's "peculiar treasure" above others. Do you get the sense or the heart of God here? God has literally purchased us to be what He wants us to be. Paul says in 1 Corinthians 6:20,

> *"For ye are bought with a price: therefore glorify God in your body, and in your spirit, which are God's."*

SEPARATION

If I really believe the Word of God, then I know that I must make any decision in my life with the understanding that it must be according to what God would desire from me. This does not mean that we become weird or obnoxious. I believe you can be normal and still be a Christian. Teenager, God has great plans for your life, and you are part of His family. I remember many times hearing my parents tell me, "Kurt, Copelands don't act like that!" Usually, that statement was made after I had done something that I knew I should not have done, and I was facing the lecture and impending punishment. I am sure you are a much more obedient teen than I was, and you probably have not been in that same situation, but I have—more times than I would like to admit. There was one occasion when I wanted to answer my parents and say, "Obviously, Copelands do those things because I just did." However, better wisdom prevailed, and I enjoy life, so I kept my mouth shut! Their point was not that Copelands did not do those things, but that Copelands should not do those things. Teenager, you are a Christian! That term literally means, "little Christ" or "Christ-like." The Bible follows that thought by saying in II Corinthians 6:17,

> *"Wherefore come out from among them, and be ye separate, saith the Lord, and*

Not Just Your Mommy and Daddy's Religion

touch not the unclean thing; and I will receive you,"

God literally tells us that we are not to be like the world. We are not to look like the world, act like the world, talk like the world, indulge in the world's vices, or pattern our goals after the things of the world. I know, this is not a popular message in today's churches, but that does not change what God's Word teaches. I guess the choice boils down to a decision that each one of us must make in our lives for ourselves–am I willing to obey Christ in the matter of personal separation, or am I going to follow the pattern of this world? As a parent, I know my daughters must make this important decision on their own. They can abstain from the things of the world as a child by saying "Because Mommy and Daddy say so." However, as an older teen, what a joy it is when my children say that the most important thing in their life is to live their life for our Saviour. Forsaking the world and following Christ simply out of love for Him. That is what Paul was saying in II Corinthians 5:14,

"For the love of Christ constraineth us; because we thus judge, that if one died for all, then were all dead."

SEPARATION

God is commanding us not to be like the world, but rather to be more like Christ. Romans 12:2 says the same basic principle:

> *"And be not conformed to this world: but be ye transformed by the renewing of your mind, that ye may prove what is that good, and acceptable, and perfect, will of God."*

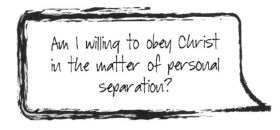

Teenager, you have an enemy that absolutely hates you. He wants to destroy your life. Satan is working overtime in your life to keep you from accomplishing what God has planned for your life. Satan knows that if he can get you sidetracked from being more like Christ and tempt you to be more like the world, then he has won. There are many teenagers who have grown up in godly Christian homes, and learned verse after verse about the importance of being less like the world and more like Christ, that no longer even attend church. There are many more who have started attending the "come as you are" type of churches and will never accomplish what they could have for Christ. Again, I am not bashing on those people; the Lord knows I have had many of the

Not Just Your Mommy and Daddy's Religion

teens through our church's youth ministry that are now in churches like that. I love those teens; I just wish I would have done a better job teaching them this basic doctrine of the Bible.

One of my favorite passages of the Bible is found in II Corinthians 6:13-18 which says,

> *"Now for a recompence in the same, (I speak as unto my children,) be ye also enlarged. Be ye not unequally yoked together with unbelievers: for what fellowship hath righteousness with unrighteousness? and what communion hath light with darkness? And what concord hath Christ with Belial? or what part hath he that believeth with an infidel? And what agreement hath the temple of God with idols? for ye are the temple of the living God; as God hath said, I will dwell in them, and walk in them; and I will be their God, and they shall be my people. Wherefore come out from among them, and be ye separate, saith the Lord, and touch not the unclean thing; and I will receive you, And will be a Father unto you, and ye shall be my sons and daughters, saith the Lord Almighty."*

You see, young person, you belong to God; you are not your own! You could put on that t-shirt that says "PROPERTY OF GOD." You are God's! God owns you because He made you. He is the one who has put into you the "breath of life." You are alive today because God has allowed it to be that way. Teenager, in spite of what you may have been taught in science class at school, you did not evolve from some monkey; you are a perfect design by God Almighty! There was not a "BIG BANG" and poof, there you were; that is crazy teaching—not to mention false teaching. The Bible clearly teaches that you were specifically made exactly how God wanted to make you. God does not make junk. So you belong to God because He created you, but you also belong to God because He bought you. The Bible teaches that God sent His only Son, Jesus Christ into the world to die for your sins and mine. We have been bought with a price, and that price was the blood and death of Jesus on the cross. You are God's twice—He created you, and He bought you! You don't have the right to do "what you want to do." Because God has done so much for me, I want to do what He wants me to do. I want to be *"unspotted from the world"* as the Bible says in James 1:27.

I am reminded of the illustration of the little boy who made himself a little boat. He carved it out of a little block of wood and spent hours carving and painting. He even made a little mast and tied a little cloth sail on the mast. He was so proud of that little boat. He put it on a little shelf

Not Just Your Mommy and Daddy's Religion

near his bed and each night would stare at that boat and dream about putting his boat in some water. One day his mom took him out to a little creek and let him put that boat into the water. He had so much fun blowing air into that sail and watching it float. The next day his mom gave him permission to go back to the same creek alone and float his boat. He was so excited and ran with his boat down to the creek. He was having so much fun sailing his boat that day that the time got away from him. Before long, it was starting to get a little dark and somewhat windy. Sure enough the wind blew by and caught that little boat and pushed it down the creek. The boy followed as far as he could, but eventually lost his little boat. He ran home crying and told his mom the entire story. About a week later, the boy

> Too many call themselves Christians yet look, talk, and act like the world.

was downtown in that small community and saw in the window of a little pawn shop his little boat. He ran inside the store and told the worker that the boat in the window was his boat. The manager came up and told the boy that he could have the boat back, but he would have to pay for it. He was so disappointed, but yet excited that he found his boat. He ran home and told his mom. She instructed him on how he could earn some money to buy his boat back, so he went to work. Just a few days later, he had earned the necessary money and ran back to the store to buy his boat. When he got there, the manager told him the boat had already been sold . . . just kidding, I was just checking to see if you were really reading this book! He actually was able to buy back his boat. As he was walking out of the store, the manager heard the little boy say to that little boat, "Now you are mine twice, I made you, and now I have bought you back." Teenager that is just what God did for us! He made us, and he bought us back with the blood of His own Son, Jesus.

We have far too many teenagers who want to call themselves Christians, yet look like, talk like, and act like the world. I love being around teenagers who love God so much that they would do anything for Him—teenagers that want to make sure that Jesus is seen in their life. Teenager, how are you in this matter of separation from the world? This is one of those Baptist Distinctives that truly does set us apart from other denominations and churches (even many other Baptist churches). Let me ask you (and please search your own heart, don't try to justify away decisions or compare yourself with anyone else) what does the world see when they look at you? When I was a teen, I remember singing the song with the following lyrics: "When the world looks at me, do they see Jesus? When the world

Not Just Your Mommy and Daddy's Religion

looks at me what do they see? Do they see hope? Do they see love? Do they see charity? When the world looks at me, what do they see?" Critics will tell you that this teaching is not important or simply "old school." However, it is very much a Bible doctrine that must be taught to our youth. Matthew 5:16 still says,

> *"Let your light so shine before men, that they may see your good works, and glorify your Father which is in heaven."*

The world needs to see Jesus in your life. You may be the only Bible someone will ever read; let it be a good copy of the Bible. Live a holy, separated life before God, and watch Him bless and use you in some miraculous ways.

CHAPTER 7
THE TWO OFFICES
Follow the Leader

Honestly, one of my favorite games growing up was the game follow the leader. I remember going to all extremes to play that game with great dedication and carefulness. I would watch even the smallest mannerisms and moves to make sure I could do it with the best of them. Sometimes I would practice on my brother Kelly. I believe my

THE TWO OFFICES

parents had a different term for that–mocking. I received many bruises following those "follow the leader episodes" with my brother. He did not seem to find much humor in me repeating every word that came out of his mouth, but I sure did–well, until he decided to hurt me. But the principle is still the same: we are all following someone. We all have those around us that we want to be just like in some way or another. It may be the most popular kid in your class at school, or it may be the person that has the most athletic ability, or simply the one that seems to make all those around them laugh. Let me ask you first, who are you following in your life today? It may be that you are following some godly leaders and striving to do what is right. As a teen, I remember friends that would put a poster up on their wall of a famous sports personality or an actor. I even remember seeing music artists and bands on the walls of some of my friends. It may not be quite as popular to put the posters on the wall as it used to be, but we all still follow and look up to someone. I firmly believe that you would be greatly benefited by striving to follow the leadership that God has placed in your life, in particular, your pastor.

THE OFFICE OF THE PASTOR

The Bible teaches of two positions or offices in the church, the pastor and the deacon. As discussed in a previous chapter, I Timothy 3:2-7 lists out the qualifications of the pastor/bishop,

> *"A bishop then must be blameless, the husband of one wife, vigilant, sober, of good behaviour, given to hospitality, apt to teach; Not given to wine, no striker, not greedy of filthy lucre; but patient, not a brawler, not covetous; One that ruleth well his own house, having his children in subjection with all gravity; (For if a man know not how to rule his own house, how shall he take care of the church of God?) Not a novice, lest being lifted up with pride he fall into the condemnation of the devil. Moreover he must have a good report of them which are without; lest he fall into reproach and the snare of the devil."*

As you can tell, there is a lot expected of the pastor of your church. This position is not one that should be entered into without a clear leading from God. There is nothing easy about being the pastor of a group of people. In an attempt to get you to understand the importance of the leadership in the church, I am listing Scripture for you to study. Titus 1:5-11,

> *"Or this cause left I thee in Crete, that thou shouldest set in order the things*

that are wanting, and ordain elders in every city, as I had appointed thee: If any be blameless, the husband of one wife, having faithful children not accused of riot or unruly. For a bishop must be blameless, as the steward of God; not selfwilled, not soon angry, not given to wine, no striker, not given to filthy lucre; But a lover of hospitality, a lover of good men, sober, just, holy, temperate; Holding fast the faithful word as he hath been taught, that he may be able by sound doctrine both to exhort and to convince the gainsayers. For there are many unruly and vain talkers and deceivers, specially they of the circumcision: Whose mouths must be stopped, who subvert whole houses, teaching things which they ought not, for filthy lucre's sake."

Here God gives us another list very similar to the first. These are qualifications set by God to be a pastor. Webster defines *qualifications* as:

a. a quality or skill that fits a person (as for an office) [the applicant with the best qualifications]

b. a condition or standard that must be complied with (as for the attainment of a privilege) [a qualification for membership]

Not Just Your Mommy and Daddy's Religion

Based on the Word of God, your pastor is called by God for the church that you attend, and he was placed there by God Himself. There are many who want to criticize and nit-pick the pastor to death. They feel it is their duty as a church member to keep the pastor humble. Let me just say teenager, that is not what God has intended. The Bible specifically says to do all things without murmuring and disputing. I have found it is so easy to complain about what others are doing while all I am doing is standing around watching. Typically, the person that is complaining is not reading his Bible like he should and he is certainly not following the leading of the Holy Spirit in his life. Learn now to love your pastor and support him every chance you get. Strive to remember his birthday and anniversary. You don't even have to get him anything "big" for his special days, but just a hand-written note or card of encouragement will mean the world to your pastor.

What you may not understand yet is that one of the most demanding callings in the world is that of a pastor. He

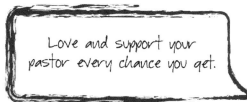

Love and support your pastor every chance you get.

is the one that is at the hospital for the births and rejoices with the happy parents. He is the one that is there to lead that same child to the Lord.

He is the one who baptizes that same child. Many times throughout the week, he studies and prays to prepare sermons to preach that will instruct that child on how to live for God. He is the one who will counsel with the family to help them through the hard times of life and the struggles that come to every family. The pastor is there to rejoice when that child graduates from high school and college. He is the one that is there to help in the wedding of that same young person. The pastor is there to console and encourage the family when death comes knocking on that family's door. He bears the burdens of not just that one family, but of each family in that church. He knocks on doors, makes hospital visits, writes letters, prepares sermons, counsels families, and motivates volunteers in the ministry. All this work is done for these families, and usually without a single word of appreciation. For every thank you your pastor receives, he will probably get ten complaints. Actually, what your pastor is used to hearing is the complaints of disgruntled families and murmurings from backslidden Christians. Your pastor needs to hear from you. Instead of complaining about your pastor, encourage him. You really don't understand what your letter of encouragement will mean to your pastor. You may think he won't even care, but I want to assure you that anytime you take the time to encourage anyone, it is worth it. Get out a piece

Not Just Your Mommy and Daddy's Religion

of paper today, and write your pastor a note to say thank you for all he does for you.

God has blessed me with an incredible pastor. I thank God for my pastor every day. I am trying to teach my children to do the same thing. I know he is not perfect (neither are you, teenager, and neither am I), but I do know that he is God's man for my church. God has called him to be the pastor of Franklin Road Baptist Church. I am going to support him and follow his leadership without hesitation. By the way, I am not talking about worshiping my pastor; the only one who deserves worship is God Almighty, not some human. Follow your pastor, teenager; do it without reservation. Don't complain about him or his decisions, and if someone around you decides he is going to complain about him, you should start bragging on him.

THE OFFICE OF THE DEACON

The other office or position in the church is that of the deacon. The Bible says in I Timothy 3:8-13,

> *"Likewise must the deacons be grave, not doubletongued, not given to much wine, not greedy of filthy lucre; Holding the mystery of the faith in a pure conscience. And let these also first be*

proved; then let them use the office of a deacon, being found blameless. Even so must their wives be grave, not slanderers, sober, faithful in all things. Let the deacons be the husbands of one wife, ruling their children and their own houses well. For they that have used the office of a deacon well purchase to themselves a good degree, and great boldness in the faith which is in Christ Jesus."

These are the qualifications of the office of a deacon. If you will notice, they are similar to that of the pastor. There is to be a high regard for the deacons in your church. The definition of the word *deacon* according to the Webster's Dictionary is "a servant or minister, a minister of the church." They are basically "servant leaders." They are to be those in the church that lead the way in servanthood. They are the ones who are to come alongside the pastor and help make his load lighter. When I think of the work of the deacons, I get a great picture in my mind of Aaron and Hur in Exodus chapter 17 when these two men held up the arms of Moses as the children of Israel fought against the army of the Amalekites. A deacon ought to support and uphold the leadership of the pastor as the under-shepherd of the church. They are to be men of great reputations according to Acts 6:1-6 which says,

Not Just Your Mommy and Daddy's Religion

"And in those days, when the number of the disciples was multiplied, there arose a murmuring of the Grecians against the Hebrews, because their widows were neglected in the daily ministration. Then the twelve called the multitude of the disciples unto them, and said, It is not reason that we should leave the word of God, and serve tables. Wherefore, brethren, look ye out among you seven men of honest report, full of the Holy Ghost and wisdom, whom we may appoint over this business. But we will give ourselves continually to prayer, and to the ministry of the word. And the saying pleased the whole multitude: and they chose Stephen, a man full of faith and of the Holy Ghost, and Philip, and Prochorus, and Nicanor, and Timon, and Parmenas, and Nicolas a proselyte of Antioch: Whom they set before the apostles: and when they had prayed, they laid their hands on them."

Deacons are to be the first to teach in the Sunday school classes and to sing in the choir (if they can carry a tune, otherwise stick to singing in the shower). They should be the men that show up for soul winning and drive the church bus. They are the servant-leaders in any capacity in the work of the local church. A deacon is not a paid employee of the church, but rather a volunteer leader appointed by the pastor. The deacons may have a secular job, but they dedicate their lives to be a servant in the House of God.

I believe it ought to be the desire of every teenage young man to want to be in the position of a preacher or a deacon as they get older. If God has not called you to be a preacher, then strive to become a deacon. What a great opportunity for you to serve the Lord. I believe a deacon ought to support the pastor publically and privately. If there is an "issue" with the pastor, obviously it must be dealt with, but otherwise support must be given to the God-appointed leader of the church, the pastor.

> It should be the desire of every young man to want to be a pastor or a deacon.

Let me remind you teenager of Hebrews 13:17,

> "Obey them that have the rule over you, and submit yourselves: for they watch for your souls, as they that must give account, that they may do it with joy, and not with grief: for that is unprofitable for you."

Follow the leader! Love the leaders that God has placed over you in the ministry, and serve

Not Just Your Mommy and Daddy's Religion

the Lord by serving with them. One of the areas that sets us apart from other denominations is this area of the two offices, the pastor and the deacon. The Bible teaches clearly that they are to be the *"husbands of one wife,"* which would mean they are to be men. Some differ with us on that, and again, I am not attacking them, just simply saying what the Bible teaches. They are to *"rule well their own house,"* they are not to drink alcohol *("not given to wine")*. God has specific guidelines for your pastor. Let me encourage you to fall in behind his leadership and play follow the leader. However, you may never fill the position of pastor or deacon in your church. Can I encourage you that the requirements that God places on these two positions are also good qualifications in general for each of us. Make this chapter practical in your life today. Young man, do you qualify today to be a pastor or deacon (that does not mean you need to go out and get married today)? You can have the testimony today of being a servant in your church–guy or girl. Begin today to hold yourself to a higher standard and serve those around you.

CHAPTER 8
SALVATION
God's Gift of Grace Through Faith Alone or Merry Christmas

I have never been one who wants people to give me things for no apparent reason. I like to do things myself. There have been some jobs around the house that maybe I should have hired someone to come to my home to do, but I chose to put on my Chicago Cubs tool belt and tackle them myself. In some cases, I wish I could have gone back and saved myself the time and money because I had to have someone come and fix an even bigger mess in the long run. There have been occasions where people have volunteered to come and do things for me. I have plenty of teens that have said they would come and mow my grass for me. But that is something I feel I should do, not to mention that I really enjoy mowing my yard. I just don't like for people to go out of their way to do something that I should be doing myself.

When it comes to this matter of salvation, however, that is something that we all must realize that God has done for us, and there is absolutely nothing we can do to earn the right to spend even a single day in Heaven, not to mention all eternity. The Bible is very clear in Ephesians 2:8-9 when it says,

> *"For by grace are ye saved through faith; and that not of yourselves: it is the gift of God: Not of works, lest any man should boast."*

That simply means you cannot get there by being the best person you could possibly be. I know you already know that, but teenager, let me encourage you to rejoice in the fact that Jesus paid your sin debt. Did you hear that? Jesus died on the cross to pay for all the wrong that you have ever done or ever will do in the future. That thought alone motivates me in a great way. I serve God because that is the least I could do to show Him my love and appreciation for all He has done for me. Although, this is an easy concept to talk about, it is a whole different ball game to practice it. Let me set the record straight teenager, I LOVE GOD! I mean I really, really love Him! He is my Saviour and King. There is no job too little or low that I would not do for Jesus Christ.

It was the summer of 1997. I had been the youth pastor at my home church

> Jesus died on the cross to pay for all the wrong you have ever done.

now for three full years, and I was having the time of my life living my childhood dreams. My wife and I took a group of teens that were part of a travelling singing group in our church called the "Teen Tones" on a singing tour up through Virginia, West Virginia, and Ohio. The trip was about ten days long and we were in about seven different churches during the trip. The group sang and I would preach. We had one afternoon of free time and took the time to go canoeing. Let me just say, getting in a canoe is not one of my favorite activities. This was going to be a seven-mile canoe trip that they said would take about six hours to complete. Along the way, the

SALVATION

water was about knee-deep in the deepest places. The water was not really moving much at all, which means it was a lot of work rowing. When we finally were getting to the end of the seven-mile trip, we were all totally worn out from the work of canoeing. However, there was one young man with us going into the eleventh grade–his name was Casey. Casey was a great young man. He felt the need of making sure everyone got dunked before docking each boat. I remember clearly as I watched him dunking boat after boat of teens as they approached the dock that day. The problem was there were about ten boats and the water was well over everyone's head approaching the docking area. My wife and I were in the last boat as Casey started swimming towards our boat. I remember my wife saying, "Casey, you better not touch our boat." She even stood in the boat with her oar pulled up like a baseball bat to use to defend our boat. It was quite an adventure. However, as Casey was swimming toward our boat to dunk us, I noticed he was seriously struggling to stay afloat. I watched Casey as he went under the water the first time. I was not sure if he was just pretending or if he was seriously in trouble. He then went under a second time–he was obviously having a hard time. He came back to the surface coughing up water. He went under again the third time, and I knew I had to do something. I dove into the water and ultimately was able to rescue him from drowning. We both laid on the banks of that river that day crying. All he could say was, "Thank you, Bro. Kurt. You saved my life." For the next year, it seemed like Casey wrote me a note every week saying thank you and asking me if there were anything he could do for me. His parents would randomly catch me at church and shake my hand and with tears say thank you as they placed a $100 bill in my hand. They were greatly motivated by a grateful heart at what had taken place in their son's life. Let me remind you, Jesus did not just save your physical life, but He saved your eternal soul. As a Christian, you will NEVER go to a place called Hell—it is impossible. You have your mansion in Heaven waiting on you even now. I remind you of a very common verse we use when preaching to teenagers. In Romans 12:1-2, Paul says,

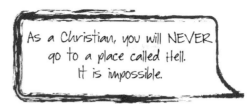

As a Christian, you will NEVER go to a place called Hell. It is impossible.

> *"I beseech you therefore, brethren, by the mercies of God, that ye present your bodies a living sacrifice, holy, acceptable unto God, which is your reasonable service. And be not conformed to this world: but be ye transformed by the renewing of your*

mind, that ye may prove what is that good, and acceptable, and perfect, will of God."

Because God has done so much for us (His mercies), we should present our lives for anything He would ever ask of us. It is no trouble to serve our Saviour when we realize all He has done for us. I love the phrase *"my reasonable service."*

I hear people say all the time that Independent Baptist people are a bunch of legalists. First of all, I don't believe they really know what that means, because we are quite the opposite. Legalism is the doctrine that you must do things or be a particular way to earn the reward of Heaven. That is what this whole chapter is devoted to, and it is one of the basic Independent Baptist Distinctives. This is who we are as Baptists. I do not serve God because I am following a strict list of rules or guidelines. I live a separated, holy life because Jesus loves me so much that He would be willing to die in my place and provide me with eternal salvation. The Apostle Paul said in II Corinthians 5:14,

> I live a separated life because Jesus loved me so much He died in my place

"For the love of Christ constraineth us; because we thus judge, that if one died for all, then were all dead:"

Not Just Your Mommy and Daddy's Religion

That word *constrains* gives me the impression of wearing handcuffs. I desire to be Christ's slave or servant. I want Christ to control my every move, even my thoughts. I love Him that much. Who, or should I say "what" do you love so much in your life today? I want to challenge you to fall in love with your Saviour.

When I read verses like Isaiah 64:6,

> *"But we are all as an unclean thing, and all our righteousnesses are as filthy rags."*

I am challenged with the fact that at best, I am nothing but a Hell-deserving sinner. I don't deserve to be called by the name "Christian." I am a sinner. It is because of that sin that we need a Saviour. I believe God when He says in II Peter 3:9,

> *"The Lord is not slack concerning his promise, as some men count slackness; but is longsuffering to us-ward, not willing that any should perish, but that all should come to repentance."*

That means He wants absolutely no one to die and go to a place called Hell. God offers freely his gift of grace to you and me. I like the acrostic of the word *Grace*–**G**od's **R**iches **A**t **C**hrist's **E**xpense. Romans 5:8 says

SALVATION

"But God commendeth his love toward us, in that, while we were yet sinners, Christ died for us."

Christ not only died in my place, but He also died in your place as well. He loves you and wants you in Heaven for all eternity with Him.

You can know for sure you are on your way to Heaven as well by simply praying and asking Jesus Christ to come into your heart and save you today. He has promised in Romans 10:13,

"For whosoever shall call upon the name of the Lord shall be saved."

That promise is for you and me. I understand you may already know you are on your way to Heaven, but if not, you can know today. Don't wait until it is too late to trust Him. It is not a matter of a long list of do's and don'ts that help you get through those pearly gates someday; it is by trusting Jesus Christ as your personal Saviour–by faith. Trust Him today!

CHAPTER 9
CONCLUSION
So What Does All This Mean to me Anyway?

You may look at this book and ask yourself, "Why did I waste my time reading this book in the first place?" I am sure some well-meaning teacher or parent gave it to you to read with the hopes that you would learn something about who you say you are as a Baptist. I for one am tired of

CONCLUSION

having the disappointment of great teenagers growing up in our good churches only to drop off the spiritual radar as soon as they get out of high school or out of the youth ministry. I want to do something about it. I want my teenagers to know why we go to Franklin Road Baptist Church.

I want my children to grow up not wondering why we do the things we do, but rather understanding what the Bible teaches and practicing it in their lives. I am tired of losing great teenagers to the worldly churches or even to no church at all.

It is my goal that you keep this book close, read it, reread it. Memorize the verses listed in this book and learn how to give an answer to those who question you about what you believe. For those who know me best, they know that I did not come up with this material by myself. There are many before me who know it much better than I do, but I love the format of the acrostic of the word *Baptists*. I need things simple in my life and any tools that I can use to help me remember things the better off I am. Take this list and put it to memory in your life. Don't just know what you believe, but master why you believe it as well. God bless you as you strive to live for Him!

> I'm tired of losing great teens to worldly churches or no church at all.

B the Bible
A the autonomy of the church
P priesthood of the believers
T Two ordinances—
Lord's Supper and Baptism
I individual soul liberty
S separation
T Two offices—
Pastor and Deacon
S salvation

ABOUT THE AUTHOR

Kurt Copeland has been the Youth Pastor at Franklin Road Baptist Church since 1994, after serving as Youth Pastor in Florida for two years prior to that. He is a dedicated husband and father who would do anything to help teens fall in love with Jesus. With a heart on fire for God, one of his goals is to never stop growing spiritually.

Made in the USA
Columbia, SC
26 July 2017